A Day in the Life:

The Empty Bowl & Diamond Sutras

Translated by Red Pine

ISBN 978-0-912887-76-0

Published by Empty Bowl Press
14172 Madrona Drive
Anacortes, Washington 98221
emptybowl.org

Printed by McNaughton & Gunn
960 Woodland Drive East
Saline, Michigan 48176

Cover and interior design by Tonya Namura
using Minion Pro

Royalties from the standard edition and proceeds from
the signed limited edition of one hundred copies, bound
by hand by the translator and friends of Empty Bowl in
the foggy November light of 2018, will be donated to the
establishment and maintenance of the Port Townsend
Meditation Center—a nonprofit, nondenominational,
community-based place for sitting and sharing the
silence. Donations can be made online at our website:
PortTownsendMeditationCenter.org or mailed to
P.O. Box 465, Port Townsend, WA 98368.

To all those who vow
to liberate all beings.

Translator's Preface

This book contains two sutras that record a day in the life of the Buddha when the Buddha was teaching the Prajnaparamita. This was the teaching that formed the basis of Buddhism's Mahayana, or Great Path, which began as a reaction to the teaching of certain sects that formed in the centuries following the Buddha's Nirvana. These "Hinayana," or Narrow Path, sects, as the Mahayana called them, believed that reality is made of dharmas, in much the same way that people nowadays believe the world is made of atoms, and that these dharmas are somehow real, somehow they exist by themselves. In a word—a Sanskrit word, they possess *svabhava*, or self-existence. This dharma-based conception of reality divided everything into form, sensation, perception, memory, or consciousness and subdivided these five (known as *skandhas*) into a matrix of dozens of other dharmas, to which nirvana and space were also added. Obviously, it was not a conception of reality that put much emphasis on what we would call "the material world." But it was a conception that nevertheless divided one's world into things. The Mahayana countered this with its own word: *sunyata*, or emptiness.

Usually when we say a thing is empty, we're negating something—something is absent that might otherwise be present. This is how early Mahayana Buddhists used this term—to negate something, not to establish the reality of something. And they only used this term in regard to one thing: self-existence. They weren't interested in negating the existence of tables and chairs or form and consciousness, only the self-existence of tables and chairs or form and consciousness. Nothing, they held, exists by itself. In fact, its very "thingness" is simply something we bestow on it. Whatever we might designate as a thing or a dharma is a convenient fiction "signifying nothing." Such an assessment may not sound like much, but if you think about it, it means that we and everything in any universe we might imagine are all of us one, or as Buddhists prefer to say, "not two." How could that be a bad thing? This, then, is the underlying teaching of these two sutras. The first focuses on applying this teaching of emptiness to all that we know—or think we know—especially as it pertains to the spiritual path of a bodhisattva, or would-be buddha. The second sutra looks at what results when this teaching is combined with compassion, with the vow to liberate all beings.

Whether what is recorded in these texts actually reflects the Buddha's own words will forever remain moot. They probably weren't written down until the second or third century, and neither made their first recorded appearance until the fifth century, when both were translated into Chinese. But in India there are still people who can recite sacred texts that go back over two thousand years and do so for days on end. So, who is to say the teaching in these texts doesn't represent the communal memories of teachers stretching back centuries earlier? My interest, though, isn't in the historicity of these texts but in their teaching, the Prajnaparamita.

This term that has become the hallmark of Mahayana Buddhism is made up of two words: *prajna* meaning "wisdom" or "knowing" and *paramita* meaning "supreme" or "transcendent." The early teachers of the Mahayana added the adjective *paramita* to differentiate their "knowing" from that of their predecessors. Unlike the wisdom of the sects that developed after the Buddha's Nirvana, the Mahayana didn't focus on the acquisition of knowledge but on the transcendence of knowledge. From *prajna*, the Greeks got *prognosis*, or "fore-knowing." For Mahayana Buddhists, the emphasis was not on a knowledge of the future, but on what comes before knowledge, on "pre-knowing." Knowledge was viewed as delusion posing as truth. Prajnaparamita was interested in the mind before it knows—our original face, as Zen masters came to call it.

The core of the Buddha's exposition of this teaching, if not most of what has survived, is contained in a set of sixteen texts that make up what became known as the *Maha Prajnaparamita Sutra*. Along with six hundred other Buddhist scriptures, the Chinese monk Hsuan-tsang 玄奘 (602–664) brought three copies of this sutra back from India. Although he was only able to translate seventy-four of the texts he brought back, they included the *Maha Prajnaparamita Sutra* 大般若波羅蜜多經, which he finished shortly before he died.

In the standard edition of the Chinese Tripitaka, or Buddhist Canon, this mammoth text takes up three thousand pages. Of its sixteen sutras, the two I've chosen take up little more than twelve of those pages (vol. 7, pp. 974–85). Not only are they short, they're connected and read as if they span the events of a single day. In the first sutra, the Buddha's disciples question Manjusri, the Bodhisattva of Wisdom, on his way to town to beg for food, and he responds with the teaching of emptiness—that anything we might think of as real is illusory and its "thingness" based on nothing more than our own projections. In the second sutra, the Buddha returns from his own begging round and teaches his disciples about what results when they combine this teaching with the vow to liberate others, all others. In using the most significant events in his own career as an example, the Buddha presents one of the earliest accounts we have of how buddhas become buddhas and the nature of the "body" that results.

The first of these texts is titled the *Eighth Occasion* 第八會 (and further subtitled the *Nagasri Chapter* 那伽室利分—after the principle bodhisattva who questions Manjusri), and the second text is subtitled the *Ninth Occasion* 第九會. Before their inclusion in the *Great Prajnaparamita Sutra*, both existed as independent texts. Two hundred years before Hsuan-tsang translated all sixteen, the *Eighth Occasion* was translated into Chinese around the year 450, give or take a dozen years, by a foreign monk whose Chinese name was Hsiang-kung 翔公. The title Master Hsiang gave his text was *The Supremely Pure Begging Round of Manjusri Bodhisattva* 濡首菩薩無上清淨分衛經, and at the end of the sutra the Buddha added another title: *The Samadhi of Realizing Everything Is Illusory* 決了諸法如幻如化三昧. I've decided to simplify this and call it the *Empty Bowl Sutra*, if only to have a title to match that of the second sutra. Before it became the *Ninth Occasion*, it was titled the *Diamond Cutter* (*Vajracchedika*), or *Diamond Sutra* 金剛經, for short. It was first translated into Chinese in 401 and has been the subject of more commentaries than there are grains of sand in the Ganges. The *Empty Bowl*, meanwhile, has yet to see its first commentary, and this would be its first complete translation into English.

Eighteen years ago, after I translated the *Diamond*, I translated a few pages of the *Empty Bowl* out of curiosity but put them aside to work on other projects. Then, earlier this year, I was invited by Jay Garfield to give a presentation about what I was working on to a Buddhist seminar at Smith College. I wasn't really working on anything and decided this would be a good time to take another look at the *Empty Bowl*. One thing that had inspired my earlier foray was that the famous verse at the end of the *Diamond* is the same verse that ends the *Empty Bowl*. At the time I felt it didn't really belong in the *Diamond*. It was about impermanence and emptiness, whereas the *Diamond* was about the opposite, namely the nature of the Buddha's real body—and the body of anyone who puts his teaching into practice. This time I resolved to find out more and made a rough translation of the *Empty Bowl* to present at the seminar. In the process, I became convinced that these two sutras are part of a whole, two views of a day in the life of the Buddha.

After I returned home, I decided to put them together into one volume—hence this chapbook. For the *Empty Bowl*, I based my translation on Hsuan-tsang's text. His version is somewhat shorter than Hsiang-kung's, but it's much clearer and not weighed down by the repetitive digressions in Hsiang-kung's text about food and begging or diversions involving billions of beings being beamed from other buddhalands.[1]

As for the *Diamond*, I've stuck with the Sanskrit. When I published my earlier translation in 2001, I relied on the standard recension by Max Muller and Edward Conze and the grammatical analysis of that text by the Taiwanese Buddhist scholar Hsu Yang-chu 許洋主.[2] Since then, I discovered that a number of sixth and seventh-century partial copies of the Sanskrit text of the *Diamond* had come to light in Afghanistan and Pakistan where Mahayana Buddhism first rose to prominence. Normally, such materials would be beyond my purview, but Paul Harrison, who has been working with these materials,[3] kindly supplied me with those relevant to my less scholarly purpose—which has been to choose among variants to produce what I consider the reading that makes the most sense. As a result, I've made changes to my earlier translation—especially

1   A selection from Hsiang-kung's version was translated by Lew Lancaster and published in 1973 in Edward Conze's *The Short Prajnaparamita Sutras*, pp. 192–96.
2   新譯梵文佛典。金剛般若波羅蜜經, 如實出版社, Taipei, Taiwan 1995.
3   (1) Paul Harrison, "Vajracchedikā Prajñāpāramitā: A New English Translation of the Sanskrit Text Based on Two Manuscripts from Greater Gandhāra"; (2) Paul Harrison, "The British Library Vajracchedikā Manuscript" in *Buddhist Manuscripts from Central Asia* vol. III/2 pp. 823–66; (3) Gregory Schopen, "The Manuscript of the Vajracchedika Found at Gilgit," in *Studies in the Literature of The Great Vehicle: Three Mahayana Buddhist Texts*, ed. by L. O. Gómez and J. A. Silk, pp. 89–139.

where these were supported by a majority of the fifth and sixth-century Chinese translations of Kumarajiva (401), Bodhiruci (509), Paramartha (562), and Dharmagupta (590).

Accompanying my earlier translation, I also included several hundred pages of commentary, both mine and that of the luminaries of Indian and Chinese Buddhism. Since then, I've concluded that for certain people, especially practitioners, sutras interrupted by so much commentary aren't as useful as the sutras themselves. Hence, in this edition I've eliminated the interruptions. However, I have added a few footnotes to make life easier for those who might be new to such texts and to highlight elements of the teaching readers might otherwise miss.

By the time I got to the end of all this, it occurred to me that the verse at the end of the *Diamond*, whose repetition there had puzzled me earlier, was simply further proof that these two sutras were connected. It was just another way of reminding us that even the Buddha's own body, the one his disciples saw, as well as the one he experienced as a buddha, were just as impermanent as ours, and that both were mere reflections of this teaching, which turns out to be no teaching.

No author works alone, and translators even less so. Before letting this go, I would like to thank Tony Fairbank, Isaac Gardiner and John Pierce for improving the manuscript. And once again I am indebted to Paul Harrison and Dan Lusthaus for saving me from my more egregious errors of scholarship. I hope the mistakes I have overlooked or insisted on making won't interfere with the reader's appreciation of these two texts from another time and another place, but one not so far away.

Red Pine
Port Townsend
Fall 2018

The Empty Bowl Sutra

Thus have I heard: Once when the Bhagavan was dwelling near Sravasti in the Anapindada Garden of Jeta Forest and expounding the Dharma to the assembly, Manjusri Bodhisattva put on his robe at dawn, picked up his bowl, and proceeded slowly toward the city.

A bodhisattva named Nagasri saw him and asked, "Where are you going, Sir?"

Manjusri answered, "I'm going to Sravasti to beg for food in order to uplift and benefit others, to show compassion to all beings, and to help and comfort devas as well as people."

Nagasri asked, "If that is so, Sir, have you not yet gotten rid of the conception of food?"

Manjusri said, "As for the conception of food, I don't see it as existing. What is there to get rid of? And how so? The fundamental nature of all things is empty. Like space,[4] it contains nothing to put an end to. How could I get rid of it? Neither devas, Mara, Brahma, nor the monks and priests of this world can get rid of it. And why not? Because the essential nature of all things is like that of space: ultimately empty, immutable, and devoid of anything to get rid of. Moreover, since everything is like space, neither devas, Mara, Brahma, monks, nor any other being can get hold of anything. And how so? Because the essential nature of everything is ungraspable, there is nothing they can get hold of."

Nagasri said, "If it is as you say, why then do bodhisattvas struggle against Mara?"

Manjusri said, "Bodhisattvas don't struggle against the drum-beating forces of Mara,[5] nor do they see the slightest thing real on which to meditate. And how so? Even though bodhisattvas might see those demon drummers, they aren't frightened. It's as if a magician conjured a hostile enemy. Despite the appearance of danger, bodhisattvas aren't alarmed, for they know that the nature of everything is essentially empty and illusory. Hence, they aren't frightened. If bodhisattvas were frightened, they wouldn't deserve the support of humans and devas. But because

---

4   Space, earth, water, fire, air, and consciousness made up the early Buddhist world.

5   Mara is the great distractor of those engaged in spiritual practices.

bodhisattvas aren't afraid of what they know to be empty, they're worthy of serving as fields of pure blessings."

Nagasri asked, "Can they realize enlightenment?"

Manjusri said, "Yes, they can."

Nagasri asked, "Who realizes it?"

Manjusri said, "Those with no name, concepts, or anything to say, they can attain it."

Nagasri asked, "If that is true, how can they realize it?"

Manjusri said, "By not thinking about it, by not thinking about enlightenment or a seat of enlightenment, and by not being concerned about other beings. Anyone who can free themselves from projections and views can realize enlightenment."

Nagasri asked, "In that case, Sir, what do you think about when you attain it?"

Manjusri said, "There is nothing to attain and no one who attains. It isn't something you consider. You don't think, 'I shall sit on a diamond seat under the Bodhi Tree and realize enlightenment and turn the wheel of the Dharma[6] and rescue others from samsara.' And why not? Because dharmas are immutable. You can't get rid of them, and you can't get hold of them. They're ultimately empty. It's by means of this thought of nonattainment that you attain enlightenment."

Nagasri said, "Sir, what you have said is truly transcendent and will surely help others who believe and understand this teaching get free from afflictions. And by getting free from afflictions, they will finally be able to break free from Mara's net."

Manjusri said, "Mara's net is unbreakable. And why is that? 'Mara' is simply another name for enlightenment. And how so? Neither Mara nor his demon army ultimately exist. They can't be found. This is why I say 'Mara' is simply another name for enlightenment."

Nagasri asked, "How would you describe enlightenment?"

Manjusri said, "Enlightenment is present in all things at all times and in all places. Just as nothing obstructs space, which is present in all things at all times and in all places, the same is true of enlightenment. Because

---

6 The word *dharma* refers to anything thought to be real. Sometimes it's simply a thing, sometimes a concept, and sometimes the truth.

nothing obstructs it, it's present in all things at all times and in all places. Thus, nothing is greater than enlightenment. What kind of enlightenment do you want to realize, Sir?"

Nagasri said, "I want to realize the highest kind."

Manjusri said, "The highest kind of enlightenment isn't something you can realize. What you would realize would be tantamount to nonsense. And how so? The highest kind of enlightenment would be a featureless nirvana. Hence, what you would realize would amount to nonsense. It would be like someone saying, 'I will conjure an illusory person sitting on the seat of enlightenment who realizes an illusion of enlightenment.' To say something like that would amount to utter nonsense. An illusory person is an impossibility, how much more so one who can realize an illusion of enlightenment. One illusion can't become part of or separate from another illusion. Concerning that which is essentially empty, there is nothing to grasp and nothing to let go. The buddhas and bhagavans have said that dharmas can't be discriminated. They are nothing but illusions. The kind of enlightenment you would realize would amount to discriminating an illusion. Dharmas can't be grasped, and they can't be let go. There's nothing to create and nothing to destroy. No dharma can create or destroy another dharma. And no dharma can become part of or separate from another dharma. And how so? Dharmas don't come together or separate. They're essentially empty and devoid of a self or anything that belongs to a self. They're the same as space. There's nothing to describe or point to, nothing to praise or disparage, nothing to elevate or debase, nothing to diminish or increase. They can't be imagined and can't be fabricated. Their very nature is quiescent and ultimately empty. They're like illusions or dreams. In the absence of anything to which to compare them, how can they possibly be discriminated?"

Nagasri said, "Wonderful, Sir! I will surely attain enlightenment as a result of this. And how so? Because you, Sir, have explained to me the most profound teaching."

Manjusri said, "Just now, I did not explain anything apparent or hidden, profound or superficial. How could it help you attain enlightenment? And why is that? The essential nature of any dharma can't be explained. Saying that I have explained the most profound teaching amounts to nonsense.

In truth, I can't explain anything and certainly can't explain the essential nature of anything. If someone said, 'I can describe what an illusory person perceives' or 'the perceptions of an illusory person differ like this and like that,' such a description would only damage their own veracity. And how so? An illusory person has no consciousness, much less any perceptions. Just now, your statement that my explanation of this most profound teaching could help you realize enlightenment is like that. All dharmas are illusory. They're essentially empty and can't be known, much less described."

While this was going on, Aparajita Bodhisattva approached and after listening exclaimed, "This is wonderful, great and noble Sir! It is most wonderful that you can explain this most profound teaching for us."

Manjusri said to Aparajita, "Great and noble Sir, what teaching are you talking about? Someone who is a bodhisattva doesn't think: 'I am a great and noble bodhisattva and can explain the most profound teaching.' To think such a thought would be to engage in sophistry. Moreover, Aparajita, can an echo speak about the reality of its essential nature or someone who hears it understand?"

Aparajita replied, "No."

Manjusri said, "All dharmas are unreal. They're like an echo. They possess neither name nor appearance nor anything you can grasp. To grasp such a thing would be to engage in nonsense. And to engage in nonsense would be to turn the wheel of samsara.[7] Things like echoes aren't knowable and only give rise to arguments. When arguments arise, the mind becomes confused. And when the mind becomes confused, falsehoods flourish. And when falsehoods flourish, the wheel of existence keeps turning. Therefore, the Bhagavan has admonished and instructed monks night and day: 'You monks shouldn't engage in nonsense. Think about the teaching I have taught you concerning nirvana. Examine it carefully and concentrate on cultivating an acceptance of nonattainment.' Thus, the Great Master of Nirvana has taught that all dharmas are empty and that their essential nature is quiescent and devoid of anything to defile or obtain or anything on which to rely. Those who can truly understand this will become free from samsara and will surely realize enlightenment and nirvana."

---

7 The counterpart of nirvana, *samsara* refers to the endless round of birth and death.

After hearing this, Nagasri once more asked Manjusri, "But venerable Sir, how do they become free from samsara?"

Manjusri said, "Good Sir, have you ever wondered how the Tathagata became free from samsara? The Bhagavan of Ten Powers has taught that the past, the future, and the present are the dharmas of samsara."

Nagasri said, "But since the Bhagavan has taught that all dharmas are illusory, in that case beings should have already realized enlightenment. Why then is there samsara? You too, Sir, have said that dharmas are unreal and illusory."

Manjusri said, "I have never spoken about the nature or characteristics of dharmas, nor have I discriminated, grasped, or created them. And how so? The nature and characteristics of dharmas can't be pointed to, discriminated, grasped, or created. Anyone who can truly understand that dharmas are illusory will have already realized complete enlightenment. But because beings are unable to comprehend the illusoriness of dharmas, they turn the wheel of samsaric existence. Just as a master illusionist can use different things to create different kinds of illusion, so too do Mara, Brahma, Sakra, along with the devas, monks, priests, nagas, yaksas, asuras, humans, nonhumans, and all the other ignorant beings of the world mistakenly cling to their existence as real. But the master illusionist knows that they don't really exist, that they are just different illusory appearances. Thus, although dharmas are illusory, ignorant beings don't understand. They consider what doesn't exist as existing and what is impermanent as permanent and discriminate all kinds of things, some according to form and others according to mind, or whether they are conditioned or not, or whether they are karmic or not. Because they discriminate things according to these and other categories, they don't really understand that they are illusory. And because they don't, they turn the wheel of samsara. If they really understood that everything is illusory, they would no longer benefit from the teachings of the buddhas. And how so? Because they would already possess them. They would already possess all the teachings of all the buddhas because their buddha wisdom would not have regressed.

"All those who can remain unshaken by the wisdom of the teachings of the buddhas know that dharmas are essentially empty. Without name or appearancè, support or duration, without anything to hold or control, get in the way or possess, they're like space. There's nothing to cling to, nothing to grasp. Perfectly and utterly still, they're free from birth or extinction, defilement or purification, creation or destruction, existence or nonexistence. Anyone who has achieved a deep acceptance of this is never apart from the teachings of the buddhas. And how so? The teachings of the buddhas have no nature or characteristics. They can't be postulated, expressed, or made explicit. No matter where there are beings, the teachings of the buddhas remain empty."

Upon hearing this profound teaching, Nagasri was overjoyed and praised Manjusri, "Wonderful! It is truly wonderful! What you have said, Sir, is so utterly subtle and inconceivable. But who can believe or understand the statement 'they are never apart from the teachings of the buddhas'?"

Manjusri answered, "All true disciples of the buddhas can believe and understand this. Whether their practice is based on faith or reason, whether they are bodhisattvas at the eighth stage,[8] or they have entered the stream, or will be reborn once more, or will be reborn no more, or are free from rebirth, or seek enlightenment for themselves,[9] or they are bodhisattvas who aren't dissuaded or deterred by the purer teachings and are skilled at abiding in the teachings of ultimate emptiness and nonattainment, they can believe and understand this. And how so? The seat of enlightenment has already appeared before these bodhisattvas, and they are able to give the lion's roar to Mara, Brahma, and Indra, as well as to the devas, monks, priests, asuras, humans and nonhumans of the world: 'I shall sit on this seat with folded legs and will not relinquish it for a moment until I have achieved complete enlightenment!' And how so? These bodhisattvas are already adept at reflecting on the teachings of ultimate emptiness and nonattainment and cannot be shaken. They are as unmovable as the hitching post of Indra. Even the strongest ox can't budge them. Thus, no one can shake bodhisattvas skilled at reflecting on the teachings of ultimate emptiness and nonattainment or distract them from the understanding they have understood or from the seat of enlightenment."

---

8 The eighth, irreversible, stage of the ten-stage bodhisattva path.

9 This refers to the four stages of the shravaka path and to pratyeka-buddhas.

Nagasri said, "What do you mean by 'the understanding they have understood' or 'the seat of enlightenment'?"

Manjusri asked, "In what does the incarnation of a tathagata consist? Where does a tathagata's incarnation exist? On what does a tathagata's incarnation depend? And what does a tathagata's incarnation realize by means of which it is said to speak and teach the Dharma?"

Nagasri said, "I don't see a real tathagata much less a tathagata's incarnation, its location, on what it might depend, or what it might realize by means of which it is said to speak and teach the Dharma."

Manjusri said, "Wonderful! Your words and understanding fully accord with the truth. It is because you have already given rise to the acceptance[10] that nothing at all is attained that you are able to say this. You should know that the same is true regarding 'the understanding they have understood.'"

Nagasri said, "But the acceptance that nothing is attained does not itself arise or cease. And why not? Because all dharmas are empty and without any nature or characteristics of their own, thus they possess no mark or surface, form or aspect. They are like space. How could I give rise to the acceptance that nothing at all is attained? If the acceptance that nothing at all is attained could arise, so could the acceptance of an echo, the acceptance of a shadow, foam, a bubble, a mirage, a hollow trunk, an illusion, a dream, an apparition, a reflection, a city of gandharvas,[11] or of space. And how so? Giving rise to the acceptance of something like space is impossible. Thus, when a fearless bodhisattva hears a teaching such as this and isn't startled or terrified, isn't doubtful or suspicious, and their mind isn't overwhelmed, this constitutes a bodhisattva's acceptance of the Supreme Dharma.

Manjusri said, "Does the acceptance of nonattainment not then differ among bodhisattvas?"

Nagasri said, "If a bodhisattva were attached to the slightest dharma, this would be the practice of attainment. If a bodhisattva thought, 'I can

---

10 For this use of "acceptance" (忍ksanti), see D.T. Suzuki, *Studies in the Lankavatara Sutra*, p. 396. Edgerton gives "intellectual receptivity" (*Buddhist Hybrid Sanskrit Dictionary*, p. 199).

11 Gandharvas are spirits of the air who build "castles in the sky."

understand the deepest things,' this would be the practice of attainment. If a bodhisattva thought, 'I have achieved the greatest acceptance,' this would be the practice of attainment. If a bodhisattva thought, 'I can accept the most profound things,' this would be the practice of attainment. If a bodhisattva thought, 'I can understand the meaning of everything,' this would be the practice of attainment. If a bodhisattva thought, 'I can penetrate all dharmas,' this would be the practice of attainment. If a bodhisattva thought, 'I can understand the nature of all dharmas,' this would be the practice of attainment. If a bodhisattva thought, 'I can cultivate all bodhisattva practices,' this would be the practice of attainment. If a bodhisattva thought, 'I can purify all buddhalands,' this would be the practice of attainment. If a bodhisattva thought, 'I can perfect all beings,' this would be the practice of attainment. If a bodhisattva thought, 'I will resolve to realize enlightenment,' this would be the practice of attainment. If a bodhisattva thought, 'I will surely be able to turn the wheel of the Supreme Dharma,' this would be the practice of attainment. If a bodhisattva thought, 'I can save all beings,' this would be the practice of attainment. If a bodhisattva thought, 'I am practicing something' or 'I have realized something,' this would be the practice of attainment. If a bodhisattva thought, 'I can practice the paramitas of charity, morality, acceptance, devotion, meditation, and wisdom,' this would be the practice of attainment. If a bodhisattva thought, 'I can practice the four subjects of mindfulness[12] as well as the other thirty-seven aids to enlightenment,' this would be the practice of attainment. If a bodhisattva thought, 'I can practice all manner of meditations, samadhis, and dharanis,' this would be the practice of attainment. If a bodhisattva thought, 'I can attain the ten powers of a tathagata, the four kinds of fearlessness, the four unhindered understandings,[13] limitless kindness, compassion, joy and renunciation, and the countless, boundless other teachings of the buddhas, including the eighteen dharmas limited to buddhas,' this would

---

12 The four subjects of mindfulness include the body, sensations, conceptions, and dharmas and are among the thirty-seven aids to enlightenment.

13 The four kinds of fearlessness include proclaiming enlightenment, putting an end to karma, eliminating obstructions to the Dharma, and in putting an end to suffering. The four unhindered understandings concern dharmas and their meaning, languages and eloquence.

be the practice of attainment. But because bodhisattvas don't practice any form of attainment, there are no differences in their acceptance of nonattainment."

Manjusri said, "If that is so, how then do bodhisattvas cultivate practices that lead to enlightenment?"

Nagasri said, "As long as bodhisattvas aren't attached to any dharma, they cultivate a practice that leads to enlightenment. As long as bodhisattvas don't rely on any dharma, they cultivate a practice that leads to enlightenment. As long as bodhisattvas view all dharmas as dependent on conditions and empty of any nature of their own and without a self or what belongs to a self, they cultivate a practice that leads to enlightenment. As long as bodhisattvas cultivate a practice without any thought of practice, they cultivate a practice that leads to enlightenment."

Manjusri said, "Indeed! So it is! It truly is as you say. Although a person dreams they travel to all sorts of places, they don't actually leave or arrive, walk or stand, sit or lie down. They don't really travel anywhere. So it is with bodhisattvas. Although they might cultivate a practice while they are awake, they have no conception of a practice. They view the practice they practice as essentially empty and are not attached to any dharma. They understand that dharmas have neither shape nor appearance, nothing to cling to and nothing to grasp. Their essential nature is utterly empty, like space. If bodhisattvas can practice like this, not clinging to anything or engaging in any all-consuming fiction, they are truly fields of pure blessing among humans and devas and deserving of the respect and support of the world."

Hearing this, Nagasri Bodhisattva was overjoyed and said, "In that case, Sir, I'm going to Sravasti to go on my begging round for the sake of others."

Manjusri said, "Go then if you will, but when you do, don't lift your feet or put them down, don't bow or extend your hand, don't think about anything or engage in fictitious nonsense, don't think about the road or about the city or its neighborhoods, don't think about anyone's age or gender, don't think about streets or gardens, buildings or houses or doorways. And why not? Because enlightenment is free of conceptions. It isn't something that's better or worse. It isn't a contraction or an expansion. It's the mind free of disturbance, language free of fiction. It doesn't contain anything to count or measure. This is the enlightenment a bodhisattva seeks. If, Sir, you can go forth like this, then by all means go on your begging round."

Due to the power of this instruction and admonition, Nagasri entered the Oceanic Samadhi. Like the ocean whose waters are vast and deep and full of all kinds of treasures and aquatic creatures, the power of this samadhi is likewise vast and deep and full of treasures of merit that nourish sentient beings and an unimaginable spiritual force that stills the three kinds of karma.[14]

Also present was Sucintin Bodhisattva. He wanted Nagasri to hurry and come out of samadhi, and summoning all his strength he shoved him. The mountains and lands throughout the billion-world universe shook six times, but Nagasri's body and mind remained unaffected and as stationary and unmoving as Mount Sumeru. And how so? Because this samadhi stills the body, the mouth, and the mind.

Afterward, when Nagasri finally rose from his samadhi, scented flowers rained down. Bowing in the direction of Jeta Forest, he pressed his palms together and with the utmost sincerity said, "I take refuge in the Tathagata, the Truly Enlightened One who realizes and teaches only what is utterly profound, essentially empty, and free from impurity or attainment, and who enables those who hear him to experience this most transcendent of samadhis."

Sucintin Bodhisattva then asked, "Kind Sir, did you not feel the earth shake while you were in samadhi?"

Nagasri said, "Sucintin, you should know that when a person's body or mind moves, things such as the earth shake too. But the body and mind of a buddha or bhagavan, a resolute bodhisattva, a great pratyeka-buddha or arhan remain still and unperturbed. For they neither see nor sense anything that moves or changes, collapses or wavers. And why is that? Because whoever bases themselves on what doesn't move or change or collapse or waver—namely what is empty and without form or the force of

---

14 The three sources of karma are words, thoughts, and deeds. In this and the next paragraph we hear the voice of Ananda, who repeated from memory this and all other sutras.

passion and is perfectly still, and who realizes that this dharma possesses no nature or characteristics of its own, and they base themselves on this dharma, their bodies and minds don't move."

When Manjusri witnessed and heard this, he was overjoyed and praised Nagasri, "Excellent! Most excellent! Since you are able to do this, go then, if you will, and beg for food in the city."

Nagasri said, "Today I have tasted the unsurpassed dharma of the Oceanic Samadhi. I no longer seek ordinary food. What I seek now are charity, morality, acceptance, devotion, meditation, wisdom, skillful means, transcendent vows, powers, and knowledge,[15] as well as the other boundless bodhisattva practices whereby I can quickly realize complete enlightenment and turn the wheel of the Dharma and liberate beings from the sufferings of samsara so they can dwell in the ultimate purity of nirvana. I now wish to pursue the practices of renunciation and to cease nourishing this vile, impure body and mind. By the power of the compassion bestowed on me by my venerable and truly pure friend, I just now experienced the most transcendent of samadhis and bow down before the extraordinary Manjusri, the unfettered Manjusri, the courageous Manjusri, the magnanimous Manjusri, the profound Manjusri, the wise Manjusri, the inconceivable Manjusri, the sagacious Manjusri, my truly pure friend."

Manjusri said, "It is excellent, good Sir, that you have been able to attain this transcendent Oceanic Samadhi and to understand that all dharmas are like an echo, a reflection, a dream, an illusion, a mirage, a shadow, an apparition, or a city of gandharvas. You should now seek to nourish the body of liberation with the boundless, measureless, unsurpassed foods of the ten powers of a tathagata, the four kinds of fearlessness, the four kinds of unobstructed understanding, great kindness, compassion, joy, and renunciation, and the eighteen things unique to buddhas. The enlightenment of all tathagatas comes from such foods, and it is by means of these that they are able to live for measureless, numberless, boundless, inconceivable, infinitely long kalpas. And how so? Such dharma foods as these are free from passion or attachment and can liberate people once and for all from what keeps them trapped and from getting free. They can

---

15 These are the ten paramitas or perfections.

also rid one of all forms of pride and free one from clinging and grasping and all-consuming fictions. Essentially empty, such foods are treasured by all fearless bodhisattvas. These are what you should seek. Don't seek the foods of the world's lesser teachings."

Nagasri said, "Venerable Sir, hearing you praise such incomparable dharma foods, I am already full. How much fuller will I be when I can actually eat them! If I should receive such dharma foods in the future, I will use the expedient means of them being no foods. And once I am full, I will use them to fill others."

Manjusri said, "Can you fill space?"

Nagasri said, "No, I can't."

Manjusri said, "Can you fill an echo, a reflection, a dream, an illusion, a mirage, a shadow, an apparition, or a city of gandharvas?"

Nagasri said, "No, I can't."

Manjusri said, "Can you fill the ocean with mere streams?"

Nagasri said, "No, I can't."

Manjusri said, "Since everything is like this, how are you going to fill anyone? Trying to fill others would be like trying to fill space, or like trying to fill an echo, a reflection, or a dream, or like trying to fill the ocean, or like trying to fill what is empty, without form, and without passion, what isn't created and what doesn't create, what doesn't begin and what doesn't end. It would be like trying to fill the transcendence, quiescence, and purity of nirvana and ultimate liberation, or like trying to fill the formless, invisible, nondual, ungraspable Dharma Realm of Suchness whose every characteristic is the same as space."

Nagasri said, "Since the foods of which you speak, venerable Sir, and those who would eat them are empty, beings don't depend on such foods."

Manjusri said, "Indeed, so it is! Beings don't depend on such foods. But if the Buddha conjured beings as numberless as the sand in the Ganges, and they all wanted to eat, which of them would you want to come eat this food of yours?"

Nagasri said, "Apparitions don't eat. Why would they come?"

Manjusri said, "Since dharmas and beings are equally illusory, no one is dependent on food. And yet beings who can't understand that everything is illusory turn the wheel of samsaric existence. They cling in vain to what might sustain them yet can't find anything that does so. Those who view beings and dharmas according to what is true—as empty of self-existence or anything real—find no sustenance in any kind of food."

Nagasri said, "But I would like to put an end to their hunger and thirst."

Manjusri said, "Their hunger and thirst don't exist. How can you put an end to them? That would be like an illusory person saying, 'I will try to put an end to hunger and thirst with a mirage of water.' You would be doing the same. And how so? Because everything is like a mirage, and every being is like an illusory person. How are you going to put an end to hunger and thirst? Among the erroneous discriminations people make, the one who puts an end to something and that to which they put an end are impossible to find. Since hunger and thirst don't exist, who puts an end to them? The essential nature of everything is already full and includes neither hunger nor thirst. What is there to put an end to? Foolish people don't understand the truth of this and think they need to put an end to hunger and thirst. Those who are wise and who can understand this truth, that hunger and thirst do not themselves exist, don't try to put an end to them. Once people understand that things are essentially empty, they no longer turn the wheel of samsaric existence. They avoid traumatizing fictions and stop making distinctions. And as far as such things are concerned, they dwell where there is no place to dwell, where there is nothing to depend on, where there is nothing impure, where nothing begins and nothing ends. Finally free, they stop making distinctions once and for all."

Nagasri said, "You have truly described the essence of things, Sir. This is truly how things appear in the Dharma Realm."

Manjusri said, "In the true Dharma Realm, things don't appear or disappear, bow or extend a hand. And how so? The true Dharma Realm is quiescent and featureless. Nothing appears or disappears. There's nothing to discriminate, nothing to imagine. There's nothing to depend on, nowhere to stand, nothing to grab, nothing to let go, nothing that moves, nothing that changes, nothing that's impure, nothing that's pure. It's like space. It doesn't move or change. There's nothing to grab or let go, nothing to depend on and nowhere to stand, nothing to discuss or discriminate, nothing that begins or ends. This is how dharmas are. Their very form is empty, their nature doesn't exist, and their characteristics can't be found. If the characteristics of any dharma could be found, the buddhas who have entered nirvana would have found them.

"Dharmas include nothing to cling to or grasp, no form or aspect, no substance or characteristic. They are ultimately quiescent. Thus, though buddhas as numerous as the sands of the Ganges have entered nirvana, not a single dharma has ever been destroyed. No skandha of form, sensation, perception, memory, or consciousness has been destroyed; no organ of the eyes, ears, nose, tongue, body, or mind has been destroyed; no object of sight, sound, smell, taste, feeling, or thought has been destroyed; no realm of sight, sound, smell, taste, feeling, or thought has been destroyed; no realm of the eyes, ears, nose, tongue, body, or mind has been destroyed; no realm of visual, auditory, olfactory, bodily, or conceptual consciousness has been destroyed; no contact of the eyes, ears, nose, tongue, body, or mind has been destroyed; no sensation that arises from the contact of the eyes, ears, nose, tongue, body, or mind has been destroyed; and no element of earth, water, fire, wind, space, or consciousness has been destroyed. Thus, though buddhas have entered nirvana, not a single dharma has ever entered nirvana. Those who would try to destroy something in order to enter nirvana would essentially be trying to destroy the element of space. And how so? The nature of everything is essentially quiescent. What is essentially quiescent cannot be further extinguished.

"Foolish people don't understand what is real and think when they enter nirvana something is destroyed. They think, 'My self and all that belongs to my self is destroyed.' But because they're attached to a self and to what others say, or know, or believe, and they're attached to the existence or nonexistence of things being destroyed forever when they enter nirvana, such people, I say, can't get free from their worries about birth, old age, illness, and death and sigh about their sufferings and lament their tribulations. And how so? Such foolish people don't understand the nature of things. And because they don't understand the nature of things, they are always arguing with buddhas or their disciples or with those bodhisattvas who deeply believe and understand the most profound teachings and who forever delight in learning and in cultivating the practice of nonattainment and who have planted good roots before buddhas in the past. Or they argue with those who possess great spiritual powers and abilities, honest merchants, and great sages. Because such people argue, they're submerged in endless nights of impurity and filth. Sages and worthies keep their distance, and those who are wise disdain and avoid their vulgar ways. They're like the dung heaps near a city or village where people and animals come and go night and day. The impurity, the foulness, the stench, the defecation do nothing but increase. Likewise, the evil, the smell, the decay, and the impure ways of fools who can't understand the essential nature of things do nothing but increase. Sages disdain them, and the wise keep their distance. Such people, I say, can't get free of the calamities of birth, old age, illness and death."

Nagasri asked, "How, venerable Sir, can we understand what is real."

Manjusri said, "Anyone who can accept getting free, embark on getting free, or approach getting free while remaining free of concepts, they can understand what is real."

Nagasri said "Who can get free of illusions?"

Manjusri said, "Precisely those who can get free of illusions!"

At that moment, Subhuti arrived and asked, "What were you two masters talking about?"

Manjusri said, "Good Sir, who are you calling a 'master?' Neither of us see anything real you could call a 'master' or anything 'talking.' Nor has the Dharma King or Sage of Sages ever spoken about anything real called a 'master.' All of this is like an echo. It isn't real. How could an echo do any talking?"

When he heard this, the venerable Subhuti entered the Samadhi of Nonattainment. A moment later, he came out of samadhi and turned toward Jeta Forest. Pressing his palms together, he said, "I take refuge in the Buddha's realization and in his teaching, in which there is nothing that is not profound or subtle, which is quiescent and hard to perceive or understand, which isn't subject to discursive thought or an object of discursive thought, and which severs attachments and fetters forever. Such a profound teaching is hard to imagine, and those who hear it are the recipients of great blessings and joy. Of those bodhisattvas who have attained that from which they can never regress, Manjusri ranks supreme. However, other bodhisattvas who have newly resolved to attain enlightenment talk with each other about this most profound teaching but don't agree."

Manjusri said, "Good Sir, you should know that in this there is no agreeing or disagreeing, no right or wrong. Nor is there anything that talks with anything else. And how so? There is nothing that can agree or disagree. And how so? Because nothing at all exists."

The venerable Subhuti asked again, "Just now I saw you two masters talking with each other about the meaning of the Dharma. Why do you say you weren't talking?"

Manjusri said, "Good Sir, have you ever heard of illusory persons, dreams, echoes, reflections, mirages, shadows, apparitions, or gandharvas talking with each other and having conversations about the meaning of the Dharma?"

Subhuti said, "No."

Manjusri said, "Since everything is like an illusion, a dream, an echo, and so on, how could you claim to have seen us talking with each other? How could an illusory person hear the apparition of a buddha talk about the meaning of the Dharma and believe or consider, meditate or reflect on anything involving name and form?"[16]

Hearing this, Subhuti entered the Samadhi of Extinction.[17]

Just then, Shariputra arrived and asked Manjusri, "Good Sir, do you know what kind of samadhi Subhuti entered just now?"

Manjusri said, "Hello, Shariputra, because the virtuous Subhuti doesn't oppose anything, he often enters the Samadhi of Nonopposition, or the Samadhi of Nonabiding, the Samadhi of Nondependence, the Samadhi of Nonattachment, or the Samadhi of Severing Attachments. When he's not in one of these, he talks, and he comes and goes, and he stands and lies down. And how so? This is because the virtuous Subhuti believes and understands that the nature of all dharmas is essentially empty and can't be found."

Shariputra asked again, "What then is the nature of a dharma?"

Manjusri said, "No nature is the nature of a dharma. And that which has no nature can't be found."

---

16 "Name and form" (*nama-rupa*) refer to what we nowadays call "mind and matter."

17 This meditative state, known as *samapatti nirodha*, is achieved prior to enlightenment.

Just then, Subhuti suddenly came out of samadhi, and Manjusri said, "Mealtime is approaching. You should hurry into the city to go on your begging round."

Subhuti said, "Good Sir, know that I will no longer go into the city to beg for food. And why not? I am free of conceptions of cities and neighborhoods. I am also free of conceptions of sights, sounds, smells, tastes, feelings, and thoughts."

Manjusri said, "Good Subhuti, if you are now free of all conceptions, why do you appear to be walking there?"

Subhuti said, "Why does the incarnation of a tathagata appear to possess the dharmas of form, sensation, perception, memory, and consciousness? And why does he appear to be walking there, bowing, extending his hand, and looking around?"

Manjusri said, "Excellent! Most excellent! Good Subhuti, you are a true son of the Buddha. Thus has the Buddha often said, 'Subhuti is foremost among those who have realized the state of nonopposition.'"

He then continued, "Good Sir, let us put this aside. I wish to enter the city to go on my begging round now. Once I have finished eating, I will go to where the Buddha is staying and will prepare some rare food for the benefit of everyone present."

Shariputra said, "Noble Sir, what sort of food will you prepare for us?"

Manjusri said, "Good Sir, the food I will prepare can't be cut into pieces and can't be swallowed. It has no smell, taste, or texture. It isn't part of the Three Realms. Neither is it not part of them. Good Sir, you should know that such wonderful food is the food of the tathagatas and no one else!"

Shariputra said, "Sir, we are full just hearing you speak about such rare food, how much more will we be when we can eat it."

Manjusri said, "The food I'm talking about can't be seen by the physical eye, the divine eye, or the wisdom eye."[18]

When Shariputra and Subhuti heard this, they both entered the Samadhi of Extinction.

Sucintin Bodhisattva asked Manjusri, "What food did these two worthies eat just now? And what samadhis did they enter?"

18 In the Three Realms, the physical eye sees objects in the Realm of Desire, the divine eye sees objects in the Realm of Form, and the wisdom eye sees objects in the Formless Realm.

Manjusri said, "These two worthies ate food free of the force of passion and entered the samadhis of Nondependence and Nondefilement. Anyone who eats such food and dwells in such samadhis no longer eats the foods of the Three Realms."

Shariputra and Subhuti then rose from their samadhis and along with Manjusri greeted the other bodhisattvas and shravakas and entered the city to go on their respective begging rounds.[19]

The venerable Subhuti subsequently came to a house in a quiet place and stood there in silence. A laywoman saw him and asked, "Good Sir, why are you standing here?"

Subhuti replied, "Good Sister, surely you know. I am standing here because I am begging for food."

The laywoman said, "Noble Subhuti, are you not yet acquainted with the conception of food?"

Subhuti replied, "I have long been acquainted with the various conceptions of food. And how so? Conceptions of food, whether in the past, the present, or in the future, are completely empty."

The laywoman said, "So they are, noble Sir. Please extend your hand so I may offer you something to eat."

The venerable Subhuti then extended his hand.

The laywoman said, "Noble Subhuti, is this the hand of an arhan?"[20]

Subhuti replied, "The hand of an arhan isn't something you can see. Nor can it be extended. That would be like an illusory person asking an illusory person, 'What does an illusory person's hand look like? I would like to see such a hand. Could you please show it to me?' Good Sister, could you see the hand of that illusory person, or could it be extended?"

The laywoman said, "No, good Sir."

Subhuti said, "Thus, good Sister, the Buddha has taught that whatever is illusory is empty. Hence, we can't talk about whether an arhan's hand can actually be seen or extended."

As the laywoman heard him say this, Subhuti's hand suddenly disappeared. As the time passed, she still wasn't able to give him any

---

19 The rule was for monks to limit themselves to begging at seven doorways each day. Hence, monks did not necessarily beg at the same doorways.

20 The *arhan* or *arhat,* meaning "free from rebirth," was the fourth and final stage of the shravaka path of early Buddhism.

food. She wanted to put something in his bowl, but the bowl disappeared too. The laywoman then walked around Subhuti looking for his hand, but she couldn't find it. A moment later, his body disappeared as well. She couldn't help but praise Subhuti, "This is wonderful, noble Sir! It is truly wonderful how you can disappear—and your attributes too. This is truly rare! No wonder the Tathagata has said, 'Subhuti is foremost in his attainment of the state of nonopposition.'"

The laywoman thereupon renounced forever the view of a self and reached the stage of a srota-apanna.[21] The venerable Subhuti then reappeared and praised her, "It is excellent, most excellent, good Sister. You have achieved something only a true disciple can achieve."

The woman was overjoyed and offered Subhuti the food she was holding. After Subhuti received it, he left and ate it.

Once Manjusri and the other bodhisattvas and shravakas had eaten their food, they proceeded to where the Buddha was staying and bowed down at his feet. After walking around him to the right three times, they sat down to one side and related the foregoing events to the Bhagavan.

After the Tathagata had heard their account, he praised them saying, "It is excellent, most excellent, that you were able to perform such great deeds. You should know that this was entirely due to the power of the buddhas."

The venerable Subhuti also told the Buddha how the laywoman was able to reach the first stage of the shravaka path by means of his transformation, and the Bhagavan praised his skillful use of expedient means.

Manjusri then told Subhuti, "The view of a self the laywoman renounced was no view of a self. Thus does the Tathagata speak of a 'view of a self.' Good Sir, this is how all those who set forth on the bodhisattva path should know, view, believe, and understand all dharmas. And how should they believe and understand them? By not dwelling on the conception of any dharma. And how should they do this? Good Subhuti, the conception of a dharma is no conception of a dharma. Thus does the Tathagata speak of a 'conception of a dharma.'[22]

---

21 This refers to the first stage of the shravaka path.
22 Finally, at the very end of the *Empty Bowl,* Manjusri gives us two examples of the

"Good Sir, you should know that if a fearless bodhisattva filled countless worlds with the seven treasures[23] and used them as an offering, and a good son or daughter memorized a single four-line verse of this teaching of Prajnaparamita and explained it to others without the conception of explaining it, the body of merit[24] earned by that good son or daughter would be far greater."

The Bhagavan then spoke this verse:[25]

> "As a star, a cataract, a spark or illusion
> a dewdrop, a bubble, a dream, a cloud or lightning
> all things that are conditioned
> view them all like this."

When the Bhagavan had finished speaking this sutra, all the bodhisattvas and monks, and the assemblies of devas, humans, and asuras of this world were overjoyed and resolved to put into practice what they heard the Buddha say.

---

linguistic pattern the Buddha will use repeatedly in the *Diamond Sutra* to emphasize the hold words have on us and how easily that hold can be dispelled.

23 The seven treasures include gold, silver, aquamarine, carnelian, nacre, crystal, and coral. The nacre referred to here is the lining of the giant clam.

24 The nature and meaning of the "body of merit" will become clear in the next sutra.

25 The verse translated here is from the Chinese, as there is no extant Sanskrit copy of this sutra. This is not the case with the *Diamond*—hence the differences in my translations.

The Diamond Sutra

One: Thus have I heard: Once the Bhagavan was dwelling near Sravasti in the Anathapindada Garden of Jeta Forest together with the full assembly of 1,250 monks.

One day before noon, the Bhagavan put on his patched robe, picked up his bowl, and entered the capital of Sravasti for offerings. After begging for food in the city and eating his meal of rice, he returned from his daily round in the afternoon. Putting his robe and his bowl away, he washed his feet and sat down on the seat set aside for him. After crossing his legs and adjusting his body, he turned his attention to what was before him.

A number of monks then came up to where the Bhagavan was sitting. After touching their heads to his feet, they walked around him to the right three times and sat down to one side.

Two: On this occasion, the venerable Subhuti was also present in the assembly. Rising from his seat, he uncovered one shoulder and touched his right knee to the ground. Pressing his palms together and bowing to the Buddha, he said: "It is rare, Bhagavan, most rare, indeed, Sugata, how the Tathagata, the Arhan, the Fully Enlightened One blesses bodhisattvas with the best of blessings. And it is rare, Bhagavan, how the Tathagata, the Arhan, the Fully Enlightened One entrusts bodhisattvas with the greatest of trusts.

"Even so, Bhagavan, if a noble son or daughter should set forth on the bodhisattva path, how should they act, how should they practice, how should they control their thoughts?"[26]

The Buddha told the venerable Subhuti, "Well said, Subhuti. Well said. So it is, Subhuti. It is as you say. The Tathagata blesses bodhisattvas with the best of blessings and entrusts bodhisattvas with the greatest of trusts. You should therefore listen, Subhuti, and ponder this well. I shall tell you how someone who sets forth on the bodhisattva path should act, how they should practice, and how they should control their thoughts."

---

26 Subhuti represents the shravaka path of early Buddhism (*shravaka* means "hearer" and refers to those who actually heard the Buddha teach), with its focus on the renunciation of desire and the attainment of nirvana.

The venerable Subhuti answered, "May it be so, Bhagavan," and gave his full attention.

Three: The Buddha said to him, "Subhuti, those who would set forth on the bodhisattva path should think this thought:[27] 'However many beings there are in whatever realms of being might exist, whether they are born from an egg or born from a womb, born from the water or born from the air, whether they have form or no form, whether they are able to perceive or not perceive or neither perceive nor not perceive, in whatever conceivable realm of being one might conceive of beings, in the realm of unconditioned nirvana I shall liberate them all. And though I thus liberate countless beings, not a single being is liberated.'

"And how so? Subhuti, a bodhisattva to whom the conception of a being occurs cannot be called a 'bodhisattva.' And why is that? Subhuti, no one can be called a bodhisattva who conceives of a being, a life, or a soul."

Four: "Moreover, Subhuti, when a bodhisattva gives a gift,[28] they should not be attached to an object. When they give a gift, they should not be attached to anything at all. They should not be attached to a sight when they give a gift. Nor should they be attached to a sound, a smell, a taste, a touch, or a dharma when they give a gift. Subhuti, bodhisattvas should give a gift in this manner without being attached to any conception of its characteristics. And why is that? Subhuti, the body of merit[29] of those bodhisattvas who give a gift without being attached isn't easy to measure. What do you think, Subhuti, is the space to the east easy to measure?"

Subhuti replied, "No, it isn't, Bhagavan."

---

27 The Buddha responds with a homeopathic rather than an allopathic solution: you don't control your thoughts, you transform them, which you do by vowing to liberate all beings.

28 The practice of charity (*dana*) is the first of the six paramitas, or perfections. While the gift that inspires this sutra is that of alms, the focus is on the gift of this teaching.

29 The *punya-skandha* (merit-body) is the result of a bodhisattva's selfless vow and tantamount to what came to be called a buddha's *sambhoga-kaya* (body of realization). The original meaning of *skandha* was "tree trunk with its first set of limbs." It was used by Jains and others, along with *pinda*, when referring to the body of the individual. In early texts, the Buddha teaches his disciples to examine the five skandhas in their search for a self: form, sensation, perception, memory, and consciousness. Here, he adds a sixth.

The Buddha said, "Likewise, is the space to the south, to the west, to the north, in between, above, below, or in any of the ten directions easy to measure?"

Subhuti replied, "No, it isn't, Bhagavan."

The Buddha said, "In the same way, Subhuti, the body of merit of those bodhisattvas who give a gift without being attached isn't easy to measure. Thus, Subhuti, those who set forth on the bodhisattva path should give a gift without being attached to any conception of its characteristics."

Five: "What do you think, Subhuti, can the Tathagata be seen by means of the acquisition of attributes?"[30]

Subhuti replied, "No, Bhagavan, the Tathagata cannot be seen by means of the acquisition of attributes. And why not? Bhagavan, the Tathagata speaks of the acquisition of attributes as the acquisition of no attributes."[31]

The Buddha then told the venerable Subhuti, "Since attributes are a fabrication, Subhuti, no attributes are no fabrication. Hence, by means of attributes that are no attributes the Tathagata can, indeed, be seen."[32]

Six: Hearing this, the venerable Subhuti asked the Buddha, "Bhagavan, will there be beings in the future, in the final epoch, in the final period, in the final five hundred years of the dharma-ending age, who think the words of a sutra like the one spoken here are true?"[33]

The Buddha said, "Subhuti, do not ask 'will there be beings in the future, in the final epoch, in the final period, in the final five hundred years of the dharma-ending age, who think the words of a sutra like the one spoken here are true?' Surely, Subhuti, in the future, in the final epoch, in the final period, in the final five hundred years of the dharma-ending age,

---

30 Over the course of many lives, buddhas acquire a set of thirty-two physical attributes that distinguish their *nirmana-kaya*, or manifestation body.

31 All subjects addressed by the Buddha are granted no more reality than the illusoriness words might bestow. Hence, any "thing" the Buddha speaks of is, in fact, "no thing."

32 With this sequence of affirmation-negation-affirmation, the Buddha establishes the logic whereby whatever he speaks of is treated as ultimately provisional. Subhuti has mastered the initial negative part of emptiness but not the second part whereby two negatives result in a positive.

33 The teaching is over but not the sutra.

there will be fearless bodhisattvas who are capable, virtuous, and wise who think the words of a sutra like the one spoken here are true.

"Indeed, Subhuti, such bodhisattvas will have honored not just one buddha or planted auspicious roots before not just one buddha. Surely, Subhuti, such bodhisattvas will have honored countless hundreds and thousands of buddhas and will have planted auspicious roots before countless hundreds and thousands of buddhas. In the words of a sutra like the one spoken here, they are sure to gain an unshakeable confidence.[34] The Tathagata knows them, Subhuti. And the Tathagata sees them, Subhuti. For they all produce and obtain a measureless, infinite body of merit.

"And how so? Because, Subhuti, the idea of a self does not occur to such bodhisattvas, neither does the idea of a being, a life, or a soul. Neither, Subhuti, does the idea of a dharma occur to such bodhisattvas, much less that of no dharma. Neither an idea, Subhuti, nor no idea occurs to them.

"And why not? Because, Subhuti, if the idea of a dharma occurred to these bodhisattvas, they would be attached to a self, a being, a life, or a soul. Likewise, if the idea of no dharma occurred to them, they would be attached to a self, a being, a life, or a soul.

"And how so? Because, Subhuti, a bodhisattva is not attached to a dharma, much less to no dharma. This is the meaning behind the Tathagata's saying, 'The teaching of a dharma is like a raft. If you should let go of dharmas, how much more so no dharmas.'"[35]

Seven: The Buddha then asked the venerable Subhuti, "What do you think, Subhuti? Did the Tathagata realize any such dharma as 'unexcelled, perfect enlightenment?' Or does the Tathagata teach any such dharma?"[36]

The venerable Subhuti answered, "Bhagavan, as I understand the meaning of what the Buddha has said, the Tathagata did not realize any such dharma as 'unexcelled, perfect enlightenment.' Nor does the

---

34 The Sanskrit term *prasada* refers here to the serenity and confidence the Buddha himself experienced when he saw his first monk and resolved to leave home.

35 A dharma is an expedient means. The Pali *Alagaddupama Sutta* compares it to a raft that helps beings cross the sea of samsara. What is "no dharma" lacks such usefulness.

36 The dharma realized by a buddha's sambhoga-kaya and taught by a buddha's nirmana-kaya and referred to as "unexcelled, perfect enlightenment" is the *dharma-kaya*.

Tathagata teach such a dharma. And why not? Because this dharma realized and taught by the Tathagata is ungraspable and inexpressible and is neither a dharma nor no dharma. And why is that? Because sages arise from what is unconditioned."[37]

Eight: The Buddha said, "Subhuti, what do you think? If some noble son or daughter filled the billion worlds of this universe with the seven treasures and gave them as a gift to the tathagatas, the arhans, the fully enlightened ones, would the body of merit produced as a result by this noble son or daughter be great?"

Subhuti answered, "It would be great, Bhagavan. The body of merit produced as a result by that noble son or daughter would be great, Sugata. And how so? Bhagavan, what the Tathagata says is a body of merit, the Tathagata has said is no body. Thus does the Tathagata speak of a body of merit as a 'body of merit.'"

The Buddha said, "Subhuti, if instead of filling the billion worlds of this universe with the seven treasures and giving them as a gift to the tathagatas, the arhans, the fully enlightened ones, this noble son or daughter took but one four-line verse[38] of this teaching and made it known and explained it in detail to others, the body of merit produced as a result would be immeasurably, infinitely greater. And how so? Subhuti, from this is born the unexcelled, perfect enlightenment of tathagatas, arhans, and fully enlightened ones. From this are born buddhas and bhagavans.[39] And how so? Buddha dharmas, Subhuti, buddha dharmas are spoken of by the Tathagata as no buddha dharmas. Thus does he speak of 'buddha dharmas.'"

Nine: "What do you think, Subhuti, does it occur to those who enter the river, 'I have attained the goal of entering the river?'"[40]

---

37 Among the dharmas thought to possess self-existence by certain Abhidharma schools—of which Subhuti was considered the founder—three were considered unconditioned, or not dependent on anything else: space and two kinds of nirvana.
38 In its original form, this sutra was said to consist of 300 verses.
39 From the gift of this teaching is born the sambhoga-kaya of enlightenment and the nirmana-kaya of buddhahood, not from the unconditioned dharmas of space or nirvana.
40 The Buddha compares setting forth on the bodhisattva path to the shravaka path.

Subhuti replied, "No, indeed, Bhagavan. It does not occur to those who enter the river, 'I have attained the goal of entering the river.' And why not? Bhagavan, they do not enter any such dharma. Thus are they said to 'enter the river.' They do not enter a sight, nor do they enter a sound, a smell, a taste, a touch, or a dharma. Thus are they said to 'enter the river.'"

The Buddha said, "What do you think, Subhuti, does it occur to those who return once more, 'I have attained the goal of returning once more?'"

Subhuti replied, "No, indeed, Bhagavan. It does not occur to those who return once more, 'I have attained the goal of returning once more.' And why not? Bhagavan, they do not attain any such dharma as 'returning once more.' Thus are they said to 'return once more.'"

The Buddha said, "What do you think, Subhuti, does it occur to those who return no more, 'I have attained the goal of returning no more.'"

Subhuti replied, "No, indeed, Bhagavan. And why not? Bhagavan, they do not attain any such dharma as 'returning no more.' Thus are they said to 'return no more.'"

The Buddha said, "What do you think, Subhuti, does it occur to those who become free from rebirth, 'I have attained the goal of freedom from rebirth?'"[41]

Subhuti replied, "No, indeed, Bhagavan. And why not? Bhagavan, there is no such dharma as 'freedom from rebirth.' Thus are they said to be 'free from rebirth.' If, Bhagavan, it should occur to those who become free from rebirth, 'I have attained the goal of freedom from rebirth,' attachment to a self would exist, or attachment to a being, attachment to a life, attachment to a soul would exist.

"And how so? Bhagavan, the Tathagata, the Arhan, the Fully Enlightened One has declared that I am foremost among those who dwell free of passion. Though I am free from rebirth and without desires, Bhagavan, I do not think, 'I am free from rebirth and without desires.' Bhagavan, if I thought, 'I have attained the goal of freedom from rebirth,' the Tathagata would not have singled me out by saying, 'Foremost among those who dwell free of passion is the noble son Subhuti. For he dwells nowhere at all. Thus is he said to be one who dwells free of passion who "dwells free of passion."'"

---

41 These are the four stages of the shravaka path.

Ten: The Buddha said, "Subhuti, what do you think? Did the Tathagata attain any such dharma in the presence of Dipankara Tathagata, the Arhan, the Fully Enlightened One?"[42]

Subhuti replied, "No, indeed, Bhagavan. The Tathagata did not attain any such dharma in the presence of Dipankara Tathagata, the Arhan, the Fully Enlightened One."

The Buddha said, "Subhuti, if any bodhisattva should thereby claim, 'I shall bring about a transformation of the world,'[43] their claim would be untrue. And how so? A transformation of the world, Subhuti, a transformation of the world is said by the Tathagata to be no transformation. Thus does he speak of a 'transformation of the world.'

"Therefore, Subhuti, a bodhisattva's thoughts should not be attached to anything. Their thoughts should not be attached to a sight, nor should their thoughts be attached to a sound, a smell, a taste, a touch, or a dharma.

"Subhuti, imagine a person[44] with an immense, perfect body whose bodily existence is like that of Mount Sumeru. What do you think, Subhuti? Would such bodily existence be great?"

Subhuti replied, "It would be great, Bhagavan. Such bodily existence would be great, Sugata. And how so? Because bodily existence, Bhagavan, bodily existence is said by the Tathagata to be no existence. Thus does he speak of 'bodily existence.'"

Eleven: The Buddha said, "Subhuti, what do you think? If there were as many rivers as there are grains of sand in the Ganges, would the number of grains of sand in all those rivers be great?"

Subhuti replied, "The number of rivers would be great, Bhagavan, how much more so their grains of sand."

The Buddha said, "I will tell you, Subhuti, so you will know. If a man or woman filled as many worlds as there are grains of sand in those rivers

---

42 The shravaka path begins with the realization that everything is impermanent. The final stage of the bodhisattva path begins with the realization and acceptance that nothing arises in the first place, hence nothing ceases. Impermanence is a fiction. It was in the presence of Dipankara that the Buddha experienced this realization.

43 The transformation of their world and body accompanies a bodhisattva's realization.

44 The Sanskrit for "person" is *purusa*. In ancient Indian lore, Purusa was the name of the cosmic being whose sacrifice resulted in the creation of all living creatures.

with the seven treasures and gave them as a gift to the tathagatas, the arhans, the fully enlightened ones, what do you think, Subhuti, would the body of merit produced as a result by that man or woman be great?"

Subhuti replied, "It would be great, Bhagavan, great, indeed, Sugata. The body of merit produced as a result by that man or woman would be great."

The Buddha said, "Subhuti, if instead of giving the gift of all those worlds filled with the seven treasures, a noble son or daughter grasped but one four-line verse of this teaching and made it known and explained it to others, the body of merit produced as a result would be immeasurably, infinitely greater."

Twelve: "Furthermore, Subhuti, in the world of devas, humans, and asuras wherever a single four-line verse of this teaching is spoken or explained, that place will be a sanctuary. How much more so, Subhuti, if someone memorizes, recites, and masters this entire teaching and explains it in detail to others. For in that place, Subhuti, will dwell a teacher or one who represents a great sage."

Thirteen: Upon hearing these words, the venerable Subhuti asked, "Bhagavan, what is the name of this teaching, and how should we remember it?"

The Buddha told the venerable Subhuti, "The name of this teaching, Subhuti, is the *Perfection of Wisdom*. Thus should you remember it. And how so? Subhuti, what the Tathagata says is the perfection of wisdom, the Tathagata says is no perfection.

"Subhuti, what do you think? Is there any such dharma spoken by the Tathagata?"

Subhuti said, "No, Bhagavan. There is no such dharma spoken by the Tathagata."

The Buddha said, "Subhuti, what do you think? Are there many specks of dust in the billion-world system of a universe?"

Subhuti said, "Many, Bhagavan, there are many specks of dust, Sugata. And how so? Because, Bhagavan, what the Tathagata says is a speck of dust, Bhagavan, the Tathagata says is no speck. Thus does he speak of a 'speck of dust.' And what the Tathagata says is a world-system, the Tathagata says is no system. Thus does he speak of a 'world-system.'"

The Buddha said, "Subhuti, what do you think? Can the Tathagata, the Arhan, the Fully Enlightened One be seen by means of the thirty-two attributes of a perfected person?"[45]

Subhuti said, "No, Bhagavan. The Tathagata, the Arhan, the Fully-Enlightened One cannot be seen by means of the thirty-two attributes of a perfected person. And why not? Because, Bhagavan, what the Tathagata says are the thirty-two attributes of a perfected person, Bhagavan, the Tathagata says are no attributes. Thus does he speak of the 'thirty-two attributes of a perfected person.'"

The Buddha said, "Furthermore, Subhuti, if a man or woman were to sacrifice their bodily existence every day as many times as there are grains of sand in the Ganges, and someone were to grasp but one four-line verse of this teaching and make it known and explain it to others, the body of merit produced as a result would be immeasurably, infinitely greater."

Fourteen: By the force of this teaching, the venerable Subhuti was moved to tears. Wiping his eyes, he said to the Buddha, "How remarkable, Bhagavan, how remarkable, Sugata, is this teaching the Bhagavan speaks for the benefit of those who seek the foremost of paths, for the benefit of those who seek the best of paths. Ever since I became aware, Bhagavan, I have not heard a teaching such as this! They shall be the most wonderfully blessed of bodhisattvas, Bhagavan, who hear what is said in this sutra and think it is true. And how so? Bhagavan, the thought it is true is no thought it is true. Thus does the Tathagata speak of the thought it is true as a 'thought it is true.'

"Hearing such a teaching, Bhagavan, it isn't remarkable that I should believe it to be true. But in the future, Bhagavan, in the final epoch, in the final period, in the final five hundred years of the dharma-ending age, Bhagavan, those beings who grasp this teaching and memorize it, recite it, master it, and explain it in detail to others, they shall be most

---

45 Whatever is a part or made of parts—worlds and dust, bodies and attributes—has no self-existence. Belief in perfected persons (*maha-purusa*) was shared by most Indian religions.

remarkably blessed. And yet, Bhagavan, the idea of a self will not occur to them, neither will the idea of a being, the idea of a life, or the idea of a soul. Neither an idea nor no idea will occur to them. And why not? Bhagavan, the idea of a self is no idea. Likewise, the idea of a being, a life, or a soul is no idea. And how so? Because buddhas and bhagavans are free from all ideas."

This having been said, the Buddha told the venerable Subhuti, "So it is, Subhuti. So it is. Those beings shall be most remarkably blessed, Subhuti, who are not alarmed, not frightened, and not distressed by what is said in this sutra. And how so? Subhuti, what the Tathagata proclaims as the best of perfections is no perfection. Moreover, Subhuti, what the Tathagata proclaims as the best of perfections is also proclaimed by countless buddhas and bhagavans. Thus is it called the 'best of perfections.'

"So, too, Subhuti, is the Tathagata's perfection of acceptance[46] no perfection. And how so? Subhuti, when King Kali cut off my limbs, my ears, my nose, and my flesh, at that moment the thought of a self, a being, a life, or a soul did not exist. There was neither a thought nor no thought. And why not? At that moment, Subhuti, if there had been the thought of a self, at that moment there would have also been the thought of ill will. Or if there had been the thought of a being, the thought of a life, or the thought of a soul, at that moment there would have been the thought of ill will. And why wasn't there? Subhuti, during my five hundred lifetimes as the mendicant Ksanti, during that time there was no thought of a self. Nor was there the thought of a being, the thought of a life, or the thought of a soul.

"Therefore, Subhuti, bodhisattvas should abandon all thoughts in thinking about unexcelled, perfect enlightenment. Their thoughts should not be attached to a form, nor should they be attached to a sound, a smell, a taste, or a touch. Neither should their thoughts be attached to a dharma, nor should they be attached to no dharma. Their thoughts should not be attached to anything. And why not? Every attachment is no attachment. Thus does the Tathagata say that bodhisattvas should give a gift without being attached.

---

46 The perfection of acceptance (*ksanti*) is the third of the six paramitas. The acceptance of nonarising was the necessary prelude to the Buddha's own buddhahood.

"Moreover, Subhuti, bodhisattvas should practice charity in this manner for the benefit of all beings.[47] And how so? Subhuti, the thought of a being is no thought. Thus, are all the beings of whom the Tathagata speaks no beings. And how so? Subhuti, what the Tathagata says is so. What the Tathagata says is true. The Tathagata does not speak otherwise. Nor does the Tathagata speak falsely. Indeed, Subhuti, in the dharma realized and taught by the Tathagata, there is nothing true and nothing not true.

"Subhuti, a bodhisattva who practices charity captivated by objects is like someone who enters a dark place and can't see a thing, while a bodhisattva who practices charity not captivated by objects is like a person with eyes at the end of the night when the sun shines forth who can see all manner of things.

"Furthermore, Subhuti, if a noble son or daughter should grasp this teaching and memorize it, recite it, master it, and explain it in detail to others, by means of his buddha knowledge the Tathagata will know them, the Tathagata will see them and will be aware of them, Subhuti, for all such beings as this produce and acquire an immeasurable, infinite body of merit."[48]

Fifteen: "Furthermore, Subhuti, if a man or woman sacrificed their bodily existence during the morning as many times as there are grains of sand in the Ganges, and they likewise sacrificed their bodily existence during midday as many times as there are grains of sand in the Ganges, and they sacrificed their bodily existence during the afternoon as many times as there are grains of sand in the Ganges, and they sacrificed their bodily existence in this manner for hundreds and thousands of millions and trillions of kalpas, and someone heard this teaching and did not reject it, the body of merit produced as a result would be immeasurably, infinitely greater. How much more so if they wrote it down and studied it, memorized it, recited it, mastered it, and explained it in detail to others.

---

47 The gift, again, is this teaching.
48 The Buddha knows, sees, and is aware of anyone who vows to liberate all beings, for they thereby share the same "body of realization," the same sambhoga-kaya.

"Furthermore, Subhuti, inconceivable and incomparable is this teaching, this teaching spoken by the Tathagata, Subhuti, for the benefit of those who set forth on the foremost of paths, for the benefit of those who set forth on the best of paths. For if someone grasps, memorizes, recites, and masters this teaching and explains it in detail to others, the Tathagata will know them, Subhuti. The Tathagata will see them, Subhuti. For all such beings produce a body of merit that has no limits, a body of merit that is inconceivable, incomparable, immeasurable, and boundless. For all such beings, Subhuti, wear the same enlightenment upon their shoulders. And how so? Subhuti, this teaching cannot be heard, recited, mastered, or explained by beings of lesser aspiration: not by those who imagine a self, nor by those who imagine a being, a life, or a soul. That would be impossible.

"Moreover, Subhuti, wherever this sutra is explained, that place shall be worthy of worship. Whether in the realm of devas, humans, or asuras, that place shall be honored with prostrations and circumambulations. That place shall be a sanctuary."

Sixteen: "Nevertheless, Subhuti, the noble son or daughter who grasps, memorizes, recites, and masters such a sutra as this and contemplates it thoroughly and explains it in detail to others will suffer their contempt, their utter contempt. And how so? Subhuti, the bad karma created by them in past lives should result in an unfortunate rebirth. But now, by suffering such contempt, they put an end to the bad karma of their past lives and attain the enlightenment of buddhas.

"Subhuti, I recall in the past, during the countless, infinite kalpas prior to Dipankara Tathagata, the Arhan, the Fully Enlightened One, I served eighty-four hundred, thousand, million, trillion other buddhas and served them without fail. Nevertheless, Subhuti, though I served those buddhas and bhagavans and served them without fail, in the future, in the final epoch, in the final period, in the final five hundred years of the dharma-ending age, the body of merit of the person who grasps, memorizes, recites, and masters such a sutra as this, and explains it in detail to others will exceed my former body of merit not by a hundredfold or a thousandfold or a hundred thousandfold or a millionfold or a hundred millionfold or a thousand millionfold or a hundred-thousand millionfold, but by an amount that cannot be measured, calculated, illustrated, characterized, or even imagined. Subhuti, were I to describe this noble son's or daughter's body of merit, the full extent of the body of merit this noble son or daughter would thereby produce and acquire, it would bewilder and confuse people's minds. Inconceivable, Subhuti, is this teaching spoken by the Tathagata, and inconceivable is the result you should expect."

Seventeen: Again, the venerable Subhuti asked the Buddha, "Bhagavan, how should someone who sets forth on the bodhisattva path act, how should they practice, and how should they control their thoughts?"

The Buddha said, "Subhuti, someone who sets forth on the bodhisattva path should think this thought: 'In the realm of unconditioned nirvana, I shall liberate all beings. And while I thus liberate all beings, not a single being is liberated.' And how so? Subhuti, if the thought of a being occurs to a bodhisattva, they cannot be called a 'bodhisattva.' Neither can someone be called a bodhisattva to whom the thought of a life or the thought of a soul occurs. And why is that? Subhuti, there is no such dharma as 'setting forth on the bodhisattva path.'[49]

"What do you think, Subhuti? When the Tathagata was with Dipankara Tathagata, did he realize any such dharma as unexcelled, perfect enlightenment?"[50]

To this the venerable Subhuti answered, "Bhagavan, as I understand the meaning of what the Tathagata has taught, when the Tathagata was with Dipankara Tathagata, the Arhan, the Fully Enlightened One, he did not realize any such dharma as unexcelled, perfect enlightenment."

The Buddha replied, "So it is, Subhuti. So it is. When the Tathagata was with Dipankara Tathagata, the Arhan, the Fully Enlightened One, he did not realize any such dharma as unexcelled, perfect enlightenment. Moreover, Subhuti, if the Tathagata had realized any such dharma,

---

49 The Buddha now turns his attention to the bodhisattva path and its final stages.
50 The bodhisattva's sambhoga-kaya, or body of realization, is created by the vow to liberate all beings. The full realization of that body, however, does not occur until one nears the end of the bodhisattva path, which in the Buddha's case was when he met Dipankara and achieved an acceptance that nothing arises or comes into existence.

Dipankara Tathagata would not have prophesied, 'Young man, in the future you shall become the tathagata, the arhan, the fully enlightened one named Shakyamuni.' Subhuti, it was because the Tathagata, the Arhan, the Fully Enlightened One did not realize any such dharma as unexcelled, perfect enlightenment, that Dipankara Tathagata prophesied, 'Young man, in the future you shall become the tathagata, the arhan, the fully enlightened one named Shakyamuni.' And why was that? 'Tathagata,' Subhuti, is another name for 'what is truly so.'

"Subhuti, if anyone should claim, 'The Tathagata, the Arhan, the Fully Enlightened One realized unexcelled, perfect enlightenment,' their claim would be untrue. Subhuti, they would be making a false statement about me. And how so? Subhuti, the Tathagata did not realize any such dharma as unexcelled, perfect enlightenment. Furthermore, Subhuti, in the dharma realized and taught by the Tathagata there is nothing true or untrue. Thus, does the Tathagata say 'all buddha dharmas are buddha dharmas.' And how so? All dharmas, Subhuti, are said by the Tathagata to be no dharmas. Thus, are all dharmas called 'buddha dharmas.'

"Subhuti, imagine a perfected person with an immense, perfect body."

The venerable Subhuti said, "Bhagavan, this perfected person whom the Tathagata says has an immense, perfect body, Bhagavan, the Tathagata says has no body. Thus is it called an 'immense, perfect body.'"

The Buddha said, "So it is, Subhuti. If a bodhisattva says, 'I shall liberate beings,' they are not called a bodhisattva. And why not? Subhuti, is there any such dharma as 'a bodhisattva?'"

Subhuti replied, "No, indeed, Bhagavan. There is no such dharma as 'a bodhisattva.'"

The Buddha said, "And beings, Subhuti, beings are said by the Tathagata to be no beings. Thus are they called 'beings.' And thus does the Tathagata say 'all dharmas are without a self, all dharmas are without a life, an individuality, or a soul.'

"Subhuti, if a bodhisattva should claim 'I shall bring about a transformation of the world,' their claim would be untrue. And how so? A transformation of the world, Subhuti, a transformation of the world is said by the Tathagata to be no transformation. Thus is it called a 'transformation of the world.'

"Subhuti, when a bodhisattva believes and understands that dharmas that have no self are dharmas that have no self, the Tathagata, the Arhan, the Fully Enlightened One pronounces that person a fearless bodhisattva, indeed."

Eighteen: The Buddha said, "Subhuti, what do you think? Does the Tathagata possess a physical eye?"

Subhuti replied, "So he does, Bhagavan. The Tathagata possesses a physical eye."

The Buddha said, "Subhuti, what do you think? Does the Tathagata possess a divine eye?"

Subhuti replied, "So he does, Bhagavan. The Tathagata possesses a divine eye."

The Buddha said, "Subhuti, what do you think? Does the Tathagata possess a wisdom eye?"

Subhuti replied, "So he does, Bhagavan. The Tathagata possesses a wisdom eye."

The Buddha said, "Subhuti, what do you think? Does the Tathagata possess a dharma eye?"

Subhuti replied, "So he does, Bhagavan. The Tathagata possesses a dharma eye."

The Buddha said, "Subhuti, what do you think? Does the Tathagata possess a buddha eye?"

Subhuti replied, "So he does, Bhagavan. The Tathagata possesses a buddha eye."

The Buddha said, "Subhuti, what do you think? As many grains of sand as there are in the great river of the Ganges, does the Tathagata not speak of them as grains of sand?"

Subhuti replied, "So he does, Bhagavan. So he does, Sugata. The Tathagata speaks of them as grains of sand."

The Buddha said, "What do you think, Subhuti? If there were as many rivers as there are grains of sand in the great river of the Ganges and as many worlds as there are grains of sand in these rivers, would there be many worlds?"

Subhuti replied, "So there would, Bhagavan. So there would, Sugata. There would be many worlds."

The Buddha said, "And as many beings as there might be in those worlds, Subhuti, I would know their myriad streams of thought. And how so? Streams of thought, Subhuti, what the Tathagata speaks of as streams of thought are no streams.[51] Thus are they called 'streams of thought.' And how so? Subhuti, a past thought cannot be found. A future thought cannot be found. Nor can a present thought be found."

Nineteen: "Subhuti, what do you think? If some noble son or daughter filled the billion worlds of this universe with the seven treasures and gave them all as a gift to the tathagatas, the arhans, the fully enlightened ones, would the body of merit produced as a result by that noble son or daughter be great?"

Subhuti replied, "It would be great, Bhagavan. It would be great, indeed, Sugata."

The Buddha said, "So it would, Subhuti. So it would. The body of merit produced as a result by that noble son or daughter would be immeasurably, infinitely great. And how so? Subhuti, if there were a body of merit, the Tathagata would not have spoken of a body of merit as a 'body of merit.'"[52]

Twenty: "Subhuti, what do you think? Can the Tathagata be seen by means of the perfection of a physical body?"

Subhuti replied, "No, indeed, Bhagavan. The Tathagata cannot be seen by means of the perfection of a physical body. And why not? The perfection of a physical body, Bhagavan, the perfection of a physical body is spoken of by the Tathagata as no perfection. Thus does he speak of the 'perfection of a physical body.'"

The Buddha said, "Subhuti, what do you think? Can the Tathagata be seen by means of the acquisition of attributes?"

Subhuti replied, "No, indeed, Bhagavan. The Tathagata cannot be seen by means of the acquisition of attributes. And why not? Bhagavan, what

---

51 The physical eye sees grains of sand; the divine eye sees the grains of sand in as many rivers as there are grains of sand; the wisdom eye as many beings as there are grains of sand; the dharma eye streams of thought; and the buddha eye sees thoughts as no thoughts.

52 The Buddha speaks only of what isn't real.

the Tathagata speaks of as the acquisition of attributes is spoken of by the Tathagata as no acquisition of attributes. Thus does he speak of the 'acquisition of attributes.'"[53]

Twenty-one: The Buddha said, "Subhuti, what do you think? Does it occur to the Tathagata: 'I teach a dharma?' Subhuti, if someone should claim the Tathagata teaches a dharma, their claim would be untrue. Such a view of me, Subhuti, would be a misconception. And how so? In the teaching of a dharma, Subhuti, in the teaching of a dharma, there is no such dharma to be found as the 'teaching of a dharma.'"

On hearing these words, the venerable Subhuti asked the Buddha, "Bhagavan, will there be any beings in the future, in the final epoch, in the final period, in the final five hundred years of the dharma-ending age, who hear a dharma such as this and believe it to be true?"

The Buddha said, "Neither beings, Subhuti, nor no beings. And how so? Beings, Subhuti, all beings are spoken of by the Tathagata, Subhuti, as no beings. Thus does he speak of 'beings.'"[54]

Twenty-two: "Subhuti, what do you think? Did the Tathagata realize any such dharma as unexcelled, perfect enlightenment?"

The venerable Subhuti replied, "No, indeed, Bhagavan. The Tathagata did not realize any such dharma, Bhagavan, as unexcelled, perfect enlightenment."

The Buddha said, "So it is, Subhuti. So it is. The slightest dharma neither exists nor is found therein. Thus is it called 'unexcelled, perfect enlightenment.'"[55]

Twenty-three: "Furthermore, Subhuti, there is nothing in this dharma that is different or not the same. Thus is it called 'unexcelled, perfect enlightenment.' Without a self, without a being, without a life, without a soul, without any difference is this unexcelled, perfect enlightenment that is realized by means of all auspicious dharmas. And how so? Auspicious

---

53 No body, no parts.

54 No teacher, no teaching, no one taught.

55 Nothing realized, nothing to realize.

dharmas, Subhuti, auspicious dharmas are spoken of by the Tathagata as no dharmas. Thus does he speak of 'auspicious dharmas.'"

Twenty-four: "Moreover, Subhuti, if a man or woman brought together as many piles of the seven treasures as all the Mount Sumerus in the billion worlds of the universe and gave them as a gift to the tathagatas, the arhans, the fully-enlightened ones, and a noble son or daughter took but a single four-line verse of this teaching of Prajnaparamita and made it known to others, their body of merit, Subhuti, would be greater by more than a hundredfold, indeed, by an amount beyond measure."

Twenty-five: "Subhuti, what do you think? Does it occur to the Tathagata: 'I liberate beings?' Surely, Subhuti, you should hold no such view. And why not? Subhuti, the being does not exist who is liberated by the Tathagata. Subhuti, if any being were liberated by the Tathagata, the Tathagata would be attached to a self. He would be attached to a being, attached to a life, or attached to a soul. Attachment to a self, Subhuti, is said by the Tathagata to be no attachment. Yet foolish people remain attached. And foolish people, Subhuti, are said by the Tathagata to be no people. Thus does he speak of 'foolish people.'"

Twenty-six: "Subhuti, what do you think? Can the Tathagata be seen by means of the acquisition of attributes?"

Subhuti replied, "No, Bhagavan. As I understand the meaning of what the Buddha says, the Tathagata cannot be seen by means of the acquisition of attributes."

The Buddha said, "Well done, Subhuti. Well done. So it is, Subhuti. It is as you claim. The Tathagata cannot be seen by means of the acquisition of attributes. And why not? Subhuti, if the Tathagata could be seen by means of the acquisition of attributes, a universal king would be a tathagata. Hence, the Tathagata cannot be seen by means of the acquisition of attributes."[56]

On that occasion the Buddha then spoke two verses:

---

56 A universal king (*cakra-vartin*) was said to acquire the same thirty-two attributes of a buddha. Hence, it isn't attributes that make a buddha a buddha.

"Who looks for me in form
who seeks me in a voice
indulges in wasted effort
such people see me not

A buddha is seen by means of the Dharma
the Dharma is a teacher's body
the Dharma itself isn't known
nor can it be known."

Twenty-seven: "Subhuti, what do you think? Was it due to the acquisition of attributes that the Tathagata realized unexcelled, perfect enlightenment? Subhuti, you should hold no such view. And why not? Subhuti, it could not have been due to the acquisition of attributes that the Tathagata realized unexcelled, perfect enlightenment.

"Furthermore, Subhuti, someone may claim that those who set forth on the bodhisattva path announce the destruction or end of some dharma. Subhuti, you should hold no such view. And why not? Those who set forth on the bodhisattva path do not announce the destruction or end of any dharma."[57]

Twenty-eight: "Furthermore, Subhuti, if a noble son or daughter took as many worlds as there are grains of sand in the Ganges and filled them with the seven treasures and gave them as a gift to the tathagatas, to the arhans, to the fully enlightened ones, and a bodhisattva gained an acceptance of the selfless, birthless nature of dharmas, the body of merit produced as a result would be immeasurably, infinitely greater. And yet, Subhuti, this fearless bodhisattva would not acquire a body of merit." [58]

The venerable Subhuti said, "But surely, Bhagavan, this bodhisattva would acquire a body of merit!"

The Buddha replied, "Indeed they would, Subhuti, but without becoming attached to it. Thus do I speak of 'acquiring.'"

---

57 Nothing gained, nothing lost.
58 Again, the full realization of the sambogha-kaya occurs with the acceptance that nothing arises, including the sambogha-kaya.

Twenty-nine: "Furthermore, Subhuti, if anyone should claim that the Tathagata goes or comes or stands or sits or lies down, Subhuti, they do not understand the meaning of my words. And why not? Subhuti, those who are called 'tathagatas' do not go anywhere or come from anywhere. Thus are they called 'tathagatas, arhans, and fully enlightened ones.'"

Thirty: "Furthermore, Subhuti, if a noble son or daughter took as many worlds as there are specks of dust in a billion-world universe and by an expenditure of limitless energy ground them into atoms, what do you think, Subhuti, would there be a great pile of atoms?"

Subhuti replied, "So there would, Bhagavan. So there would, Sugata. There would be a great pile of atoms. And how so? If a great pile of atoms existed, Bhagavan, the Tathagata would not have spoken of a pile of atoms. And why not? Bhagavan, this pile of atoms of which the Tathagata speaks is said by the Tathagata to be no pile. Thus does he speak of a 'pile of atoms.' Also, Bhagavan, this billion-world universe of which the Tathagata speaks is said by the Tathagata to be no universe. Thus does he speak of a 'billion-world universe.' And how so? Bhagavan, if a universe existed, attachment to an entity would exist.[59] But whenever the Tathagata speaks of attachment to an entity, the Tathagata speaks of it as no attachment. Thus does he speak of 'attachment to an entity.'"

The Buddha said, "Subhuti, attachment to an entity is nonsensical and inexplicable. Yet foolish people are attached."

Thirty-one: "And how so? Subhuti, if someone should claim that the Tathagata speaks of a view of a self, or that the Tathagata speaks of a view of a being, a view of a life, or a view of a soul, would such a claim be true, Subhuti?"

Subhuti said, "No, Bhagavan. No, indeed, Sugata. Such a claim would not be true. And why not? Bhagavan, when the Tathagata speaks of a view of a self, the Tathagata speaks of it as no view. Thus does he speak of a 'view of a self.'"

The Buddha said, "Indeed, Subhuti, so it is. Those who set forth on the bodhisattva path should know, see, believe, and understand all dharmas

59 The Sanskrit word for "entity" is *pinda*, which also began this sutra as a ball of rice.

but do so without being attached to the idea of a dharma. And how so? The idea of a dharma, Subhuti, the idea of a dharma is said by the Tathagata to be no idea. Thus does he speak of the 'idea of a dharma.'"

Thirty-two: "Furthermore, Subhuti, if a fearless bodhisattva filled measureless, infinite worlds with the seven treasures and gave them as an offering, and a noble son or daughter took but a single four-line verse of this teaching of Prajnaparamita and memorized it, made it known, recited it, mastered it, and explained it in detail to others, the body of merit produced as a result by that noble son or daughter would be immeasurably, infinitely greater. And how should they explain it? By not explaining. Thus should they explain it.

> "As a lamp, a cataract, a shooting star
> an illusion, a dewdrop, a bubble
> a dream, a cloud, a flash of lightning
> view all conditioned things like this."

All this was spoken by the Buddha to the delight of the elder Subhuti. And with what the Buddha said, the monks and nuns, laymen and laywomen, and all the devas, humans, asuras, and gandharvas of the world were also greatly pleased.

Thus ends the Holy Diamond Cutting Prajnaparamita and Mother of Buddhas.